Enhancing motivation an
throughout the lifespan

Susan Hallam

First published in 2005 by the Institute of Education, University of London,
20 Bedford Way, London WC1H 0AL
www.ioe.ac.uk/publications

Over 100 years of excellence in education

© Institute of Education, University of London 2005

Susan Hallam asserts the moral right to be identified as the author of this work.

All rights reserved. No part of this publication may be reproduced, stored in a retrieval system, or transmitted in any form or by any means, electronic, mechanical, photocopying, recording or otherwise, without the prior permission of the copyright owner.

British Library Cataloguing in Publication Data:

A catalogue record for this publication is available from the British Library

ISBN 0 85473 722 7

Design by Andrew Chapman

Page make-up and printing by the Alden Group, Oxford

Institute of Education • University of London

Enhancing motivation and learning throughout the lifespan

Susan Hallam

Professor of Education

Based on a Professorial Lecture delivered at the Institute of Education, University of London on 25 May 2005

Professor Susan Hallam

Enhancing motivation and learning throughout the lifespan

Learning

Learning is a natural process for human beings (Newell, 1990). We are pre-programmed to learn. In our everyday lives, during our interactions with others and with the environment, we are constantly engaged in learning. This may be deliberate and intentional, or incidental and without conscious awareness. All forms of learning share one common element – they involve change in the individual learner. This change is sometimes observable in behaviour, but not always. Typically, we think of learning as the deliberate acquisition of skills or knowledge, but learning occurs in relation to emotions, attitudes and beliefs, including those about ourselves. Whether what we have learned is retained in the long term depends on the extent of our ongoing engagement with it and how important it is to us. Indeed, whether we attend to particular stimuli in the environment at all depends on the brain's assessment of the extent to which they might be important to us. Central to the unconscious selection of what to attend to and what to learn is the self, which itself is learned and developed through our interactions with others. The self is also central to our conscious motivation to learn. It plays a central role in determining what we want to learn, how we go about learning it and whether we persist in learning.

What is the role of the teacher in learning? Teaching has been viewed in many different ways, for instance as clinical problem solving (Kagan, 1988), a cognitive skill (Leinhardt and Greeno, 1986), craft knowledge (Leinhardt, 1990), management (Biggs and Telfer, 1987), apprenticeship (Pratt, 1992), transaction (Barnes, 1976), and guided participation (Rogoff, 1990). It has also been conceptualised on a continuum from the transmission of knowledge at one end to the facilitation of learning at the other (Kember, 1997). However one views teaching, what is inescapable is that teachers cannot learn for their students. They can support learning in a variety of ways, but ultimately it is the learner who has to engage with the learning process. To do this, learners need to be motivated. This lecture explores what we know about learning and motivation and how educators across all phases of compulsory education and beyond might enhance their students' motivation and hence their learning.

What can studies of the brain tell us about learning?

Although our knowledge of the way the brain works is in its infancy, some of the fundamental processes involved in learning have been established. The human brain contains approximately 100 billion neurons, each of which has considerable processing capacity (some estimates suggest each is the equivalent of a modest-sized computer). A considerable proportion of the 100 billion neurons are active simultaneously and information processing is undertaken largely through interactions between them, each having approximately a thousand connections with other neurons. When we learn, there are changes in the growth of axons and dendrites and the number of synapses connecting neurons, a process known as 'synaptogenesis'. When an event is important enough, or is repeated sufficiently often, synapses and neurons fire repeatedly, indicating that this event is worth remembering (Fields, 2005). In this way, changes in the efficacy of existing connections are made. As learning continues and particular activities are engaged with over time, myelinisation takes place. This involves an increase in the coating of the axon of each neuron, which improves insulation and makes the established connections more efficient. Pruning also occurs, a process which reduces the number of synaptic connections, enabling fine-tuning of functioning. Through combinations of these processes, which occur over different timescales, the cerebral cortex self-organises in response to external stimuli and our learning activities (Pantev et al., 2003).

Much learning occurs without our conscious awareness (Blakemore and Frith, 2000). For instance, when we listen to music or speech, we process an enormous amount of information rapidly. The ease with which we do this depends on our prior musical and linguistic experiences and the culturally determined tonal scheme or language to which we have become accustomed (Dowling, 1992, 1993). This knowledge is implicit, learned through exposure to particular environments, and is applied automatically whenever we listen to music or speech. Neural responses to change in such stimuli seem to occur rapidly. For instance, in one study, when individuals listened to some of their favourite music from which one specific spectral frequency was removed, there was an initial change in reported perception. However, adaptation to this occurred quickly and by the end of a three-hour listening session, appreciation of the music was unchanged from previous levels (Pantev *et al.*, 2003). Similar changes have been observed in relation to the development of motor skills. When participants practised five-finger exercises on the piano over as short a period as five days, there was evidence of enlargement of the cortical representation area targeting the long finger flexor and extensor muscles (Pascual-Leone *et al.*, 1994). Where practice continued over further weeks, the cortical maps obtained after the weekend rest showed a small change from baseline, with a tendency to increase in size over the course of the study (Pascual-Leone, 2003). Over a four-week period there was evidence of the beginnings of the process of brain reorganisation.

Permanent and substantial reorganisation of brain functioning takes considerable time. Long years of instrumental music practice are associated with an increase in neuronal representation specific for the processing of the tones of the musical scale, the largest cortical representations found in musicians playing instruments for the longest periods of time (Pantev *et al.*, 2003). Changes are also specific to the particular musical learning undertaken (Munte *et al.*, 2003). Processing of pitch in string players is characterised by longer surveillance and more frontally distributed event-related brain potentials (ERP) attention. Drummers generate more complex memory traces of the temporal organisation of musical sequences and conductors demonstrate greater surveillance of auditory space (Munte *et al.*, 2003). Compared with non-musicians, string players have greater somatosensory representations of finger activity, the amount of increase depending on the age of starting to play (Pantev *et al.*, 2003;

Elbert *et al.*, 1995; Karni *et al.*, 1995). Similar findings have been reported in relation to taxi drivers, where the posterior hippocampi (the brain regions which store spatial representation of the environment) have been found to be significantly larger relative to those of controls: the longer the time spent as a taxi driver, the greater the extent of change (Maguire *et al.*, 2000). Clearly, the brain develops in very specific ways in response to particular learning activities and the extent of change depends on the length of time engaged with learning.

Particular methods of approaching problem solving are reflected in subsequent brain activity. When two groups of students (aged 13–15) were taught to judge symmetrically structured musical phrases as balanced or unbalanced, one group using traditional instructions about the differences (including verbal explanations, visual aids, notation, verbal rules, playing of musical examples), and the other group participating in musical experiences (singing, playing, improvising or performing examples from the musical literature), activity in different brain areas was observed. The music processing of the traditionally trained group produced increased activation of the left fronto-temporal brain regions, probably reflecting inner speech and analytical, step-by-step processing. In contrast, the musically trained procedural group showed increased activation of the right frontal and bilateral parieto-occipital lobes, indicating a more global way of processing and visuo-spatial associations (Altenmuller *et al.*, 1997).

Taken together, the evidence suggests that the brain substrates of processing reflect the 'learning biography' of each individual (Altenmuller, 2003: 349). As we engage with different learning experiences over long periods of time, permanent changes occur in the brain. These changes seem to reflect not only what we have learned but also *how* we have learned. What the research cannot tell us is how these long-term changes in the brain affect information processing, learning, problem solving, and undertaking creative activities. We must turn to the literature on the development of expertise to explore these issues.

Learning as the development of expertise

Research on the development of expertise is characterised by exploration of the ways in which individuals acquire specific skills and knowledge in a domain and how thinking and learning processes change as expertise develops. Developing even moderate levels of expertise in any field of study requires considerable time. Chase and Simon (1973) reasoned that to attain masters' level, chess players typically spent 10,000 to 20,000 hours engaged exclusively with chess. In music, up to 16 years of practice are required to achieve levels which will lead to international standing in playing an instrument. The individual usually begins to play at a very early age, with increasing amounts of practice being undertaken, up to as much as 50 hours a week by adolescence (Sosniak, 1985). Equally long periods of learning are necessary to acquire high levels of expertise in a variety of domains, for example in sporting activities, as a master chef, gaining doctoral-level qualifications or professional status in medicine or the law.

The expertise paradigm challenges accepted notions that high-level achievement depends on inherited ability, and suggests instead that the length of time engaged in activities is a better predictor of the level of expertise attained. For example, studying expert memory, Ericsson and Chase (1982) offered financial inducement to university students to remember sequences of random numbers. After 250 days of practice one student was able to repeat random digit strings as long as 80 items using a relatively simple strategy based on knowledge he already possessed. He grouped digits into chunks of three or four, based on codable running times for various races. For example, he would remember 3, 4, 9, 2 as 3 minutes, 49.2 seconds, near the world record time for running a mile. These chunks were then grouped into higher-level structures for retrieval. Learning depended on linking new knowledge in meaningful ways to existing knowledge, and practising the implementation of coding and retrieval strategies. Success and ongoing improvement in performance maintained the student's motivation over the period of the study, in contrast to other volunteers who dropped out early on. The strategies adopted, using systematic methods of coding and retrieving information to learn what would otherwise be meaningless material, mirrored those adopted by expert memorisers. This research not only demonstrated the importance of prior knowledge and understanding in learning and remembering new information, but also highlighted the way that motivation is influenced by progress and success.

Changes in learning and processing as expertise develops

As expertise develops, processing in the expert domain changes. Across a range of domains a number of common characteristics of expert performance have been identified (Glaser and Chi, 1988). Experts excel mainly in their own domains, perceive large, meaningful patterns in their domain, are fast, have superior short-term and long-term memory, see and represent a problem in their domain at a deeper level than novices, spend a great deal of time analysing a problem qualitatively before attempting a solution, and have strong self-monitoring skills.

Experts excel mainly in their own domains

A person highly skilled in one domain cannot automatically transfer their skills to another, because their expertise relies on the acquisition of a large body of domain-specific knowledge. Even within domains, transfer of skills can be problematic. For instance, Sudnow (1978), a highly skilled, adult, professional, classical musician, documented how tedious, effortful, frustrating and time-consuming was the experience of acquiring expertise in jazz improvisation.

Experts perceive large, meaningful patterns in their domain

The acquisition of an extensive body of domain knowledge enables experts to perceive large, meaningful patterns (Egan and Schwartz, 1979; Akin, 1980). For instance, in music, when reading notation, skilled readers do not fixate on each note; their fixations are directed across line and phrase boundaries, scanning ahead and returning to the current point of performance (Goolsby, 1994). They scan the page more efficiently and require shorter and fewer fixations to compare or encode material for execution than novices because they are able to grasp more information in one fixation (Waters et al., 1997). They can continue to read about six or seven notes after removal of the printed page, while poor readers only manage about three or four (Sloboda, 1984; Goolsby, 1994). Similarly, professional composers take a more holistic view of a composition they are working on and maintain this conceptually while working on arising problems. Novices consider only local features or isolated individual sounds, while those working at a higher level adopt a gestalt-like approach, which demonstrates their ability to consider the detail of the task within the structured whole (Younker and Smith, 1996).

Experts are fast
Experts work faster than novices. Hours of engagement with relevant activities ensure that skills are automated to high levels, which frees up memory capacity for processing other aspects of the task. This has been demonstrated across a wide range of domains, including chess, music, typing, physics and route planning.

Experts have superior short-term and long-term memory
Experts do not have a greater capacity in their short-term memory than novices, but the automaticity that they develop in relation to many of their skills frees up working memory for other tasks. For instance, DeGroot (1966) studied chess masters, experts and novices and found relatively few differences in the thinking of fair chess players and chess masters. The key difference seemed to be in memory for chess positions. The master chess players could reproduce with few errors almost all the pieces on a chessboard after a five-second exposure. The performance of expert and novice players was poorer. The masters' superior memory was specific for meaningful chess positions; memory for meaningless positions was considerably less (Chase and Simon, 1973).

Experts see and represent a problem in their domain at a deeper level than novices
The conceptual categories which experts adopt in problem solving are semantically and principle-based, whereas those of novices are syntactically or surface feature oriented. For instance, in physics, experts use principles of mechanics to organise categories, whereas novices build their problem categories around literal objects stated in the problem (Chi *et al.*, 1981). Expert programmers sort problems according to solution algorithms, whereas novices sort them according to areas of application, for example whether the programme is to create a list of employees' salaries or to keep a file of current user identification (Weiser and Shertz, 1983).

Experts spend a great deal of time analysing a problem qualitatively before attempting a solution
Experts spend time trying to understand the problem that they are trying to resolve, building a mental representation from which they can infer relations,

define the situation and add constraints to the problem. This can be seen most clearly when problems are ill-defined, for example in creative processes. For instance, Collins (2005), studying a single composer, demonstrated strategies operating at micro and macro levels. At the outset a clear mental picture of the composition was in place, which acted as a loose framework throughout the process. Problem proliferation and successive solution implementation occurred not only in a linear manner but also recursively. Moments of gestalt creative insight were observed which related to problem restructuring; some were seen to overlap in real time with others, indicating an element of parallelism in thinking. There were no clear boundaries between the various stages. For each problem arising, solutions themselves were conjectured, implemented or deferred.

Experts have strong self-monitoring skills
Experts have well-developed metacognitive and self-monitoring skills (Hallam, 1995, 2001a; Larkin, 1983). They know why they make errors, why they fail to comprehend, when they need to check their solutions, what they need to do next. They are better than novices in judging the difficulty of a problem and selecting appropriate strategies to solve it (Chi *et al.*, 1982; Hallam, 1995, 2001a).

How does expertise develop?
Three main stages have been identified in the acquisition of expert levels of performance. In relation to procedural skill development there is initially a cognitive–verbal–motor stage, where learning is consciously controlled; the learner understands what is required and carries it out while consciously providing self-instruction. Learning is supported when the learner has a clear mental representation of both the process and the goal of learning and when feedback is available, either directly from the environment or from observers. In the associative stage, the learner begins to put together a sequence of responses which become more fluent over time. Errors are detected and eliminated and feedback from others or self-monitoring continues to be important. In the final, autonomous stage, the skill becomes automated, is carried out without

conscious effort, and continues to develop each time it is used, becoming quicker and more fluent. As automaticity develops, the component processes become unavailable to conscious inspection and the learner has difficulty in explaining their actions to others (Fitts and Posner, 1967).

The term 'acclimation' has been adopted to describe the first stage of knowledge acquisition, where learners orient to a complex unfamiliar domain and are initially unable to discern the difference between accurate/inaccurate and relevant/tangential knowledge (Alexander, 2003; Jetton and Alexander, 1997). The transformation into the second stage, competence, is marked by qualitative and quantitative changes in knowledge. 'Competent' individuals have acquired a foundational body of domain knowledge which is relatively cohesive and principled in structure and they apply a mixture of surface and deep approaches to learning. Interest during this stage is stimulated by the learning environment. To move to the third and final proficiency/expertise stage, where exclusively deep processing is adopted, a synergy among elements of knowledge is required. To attain this level, students require increasing levels of personal motivation (Alexander *et al.*, in press).

Although the development of procedural skills and the acquisition of knowledge have been described separately, in practice, in most domains, the two are inextricably intertwined. Knowledge-based mental representations of appropriate outcomes are required to check for errors, to select possible strategies and to monitor progress (Hallam, 1995; 2001a; 2001b). These principles apply in relation to creative and routine tasks. While there may be some transfer of metacognitive or self-regulatory strategies, the impact of these may be limited because of the lack of relevant knowledge. An individual may have a wide range of strategies for developing understanding and supporting learning, for instance rehearsal, summarising, elaboration, organisation and repetition, but these will be of limited use unless the individual has sufficient prior knowledge in the domain to apply them. Executive strategies relating to planning, monitoring and evaluating also require extensive domain knowledge, although strategies for managing concentration, reducing distraction and managing motivation may be more successfully transferred within and between domains.

Motivation and learning

Identification of the self within a domain

Motivation and personal commitment are required to sustain the time and effort needed to develop high levels of expertise in a domain. While intrinsic motivation may be generated by interesting tasks in the short term, that interest must be internalised and become part of the individual's identity for motivation to be sustained over long periods of time. This is evidenced by research undertaken with young musicians. Sosniak (1985, 1990) outlined the relationship between motivation and expertise development in three phases: introduction to activity in the domain through playful engagement which is intrinsically rewarding; the start of instruction and deliberate practice; and commitment to pursue activities on a full-time basis. Harnischmacher (1995) provided a more detailed account of the relationship in school-aged students. In the activity stage (8–10 years), musical activity was play-related. During the adoption stage (11–12 years), the work ethic developed and the young musicians recognised causality and goal-orientation in practice. During the stage of integration (13–14 years), practice became part of the daily routine while the playful element served for relaxation. At the stage of identification (15–18 years), there was reflection on the implicit self-relation of practice, as well as improving effectiveness and an awareness of standards. Exploration of lifelong development in musicians' lives extended these analyses, supporting the findings regarding the early stages and adding later phases referring to: the formation and development of artistic personality; establishment in the music profession as a performer; the teaching phase; and the retreat from professional activity (Manturzewska, 1990). Of course, the times at which these various phases occur may vary between domains, but similar progressions seem likely.

Initial personal interest in a domain seems to develop through playful and enjoyable activities, with greater commitment being made at a later stage. The highest levels of motivation occur where the individual's identity becomes inextricably linked to the domain. Research on the personalities of young musicians has shown that those who emerged as the most highly accomplished appeared to be self-motivated almost to the point of obsession, as if they were unable to separate their developing self-perception from that of being a musician (Kemp, 1996). This level of commitment prevents children giving up playing an instrument even when they experience bullying or loss of popularity as a result of their involvement in music (Howe and Sloboda, 1991).

The role of the family

The importance of the family in promoting interest, learning and motivation in a domain is clearly illustrated in relation to music. High-achieving young musicians sing recognisable tunes on average six months earlier than other young musicians (Sloboda and Davidson, 1996). The age at which they first sing is related to the number of musical behaviours initiated by their parents (Howe et al., 1995). Families often play a role in the identification of musical talent (Rexroad, 1985) and parents of high achievers tend to have very high expectations and are demanding in the extent to which these are attained (Bastian, 1989; Lassiter, 1981). The child internalises the expectations, and achievement becomes a need in itself (McClelland et al., 1953; Atkinson, 1964). Family expectations, some based on transgenerational influences, can be highly powerful forces. The combination of the parents' family histories, emergent expectations, role allocations and current dynamic interactions within the family play a central role in defining musical identity (Borthwick and Davidson, 2002). Parental commitment to assisting, encouraging and supporting the child in the early stages of learning is an important predictor of success (Davidson et al., 1995). Interest in and engagement with music, in the home or at school, influences not only career aspirations but also adult participation in amateur musical activities (Belz, 1995; Holmquist, 1995; Chiodo, 1998; Conda, 1997). The pattern of engagement seems to change over the life course, diminishing in the middle years and increasing in retirement (Larson, 1983), life-changing events sometimes providing an impetus for re-engagement (Conda, 1997). Interest in a domain developed in childhood is likely to be sustained throughout the lifespan, as a hobby or as a career.

The influence of teachers and the school

The influence of early teachers who are viewed as warm and sympathetic seems to be particularly important in developing interest in a domain (Sosniak, 1985;

Sloboda and Howe, 1991). Relatively uncritical encouragement in the early stages of engagement encourages the development of a positive self-concept. Once this is established, later teachers provide high-status role models with whom young people can identify and whom they emulate (Manturzewska, 1990). Strong criticism by teachers has been associated with negative emotions which create anxiety and reduce motivation. In adolescence, the peer group is very powerful and can bring negative pressure to bear in relation to engagement with some activities (Finnas, 1987, 1989). To withstand this, domain-related identities need to be well developed. Where activities are voluntary and extra-curricular, the value that teachers within schools attach to them and the support that they offer to pupils is important in sustaining motivation (Hallam and Prince, 2000). Teachers can modify pupils' attitudes towards particular subjects and counter negative social influences through their enthusiasm. Their interest and competence contribute towards pupils' attitudes and subsequent attainment (Szubertowska, in press). Where teachers motivate pupils to engage with particular subjects, identities within those domains develop, leading to more positive attitudes towards those subjects and their teachers (Lamont, 2002).

Goals

As part of the process of developing and consolidating identity, individuals set themselves goals. These take account of both context and cognition. One example of such a goal is a 'possible self'. If an individual perceives him or herself as successful in a domain and attributes this success to ability, they may come to include in their self-concept a 'positive possible future self' in that domain (Markus and Ruvolo, 1989). Possible selves can be powerful motivators, providing long-term goals and encouraging the setting up of interim goals which need to be achieved en route.

Possible selves can be negative as well as positive. Some children develop negative possible selves in relation to formal education and compensate by developing positive possible selves in other areas of their lives (Koupadi, 1995). These identities, alienated from school, provide kudos with peers (Hinds, 2005). In some cases, for instance following exclusion from school, negative possible selves can dominate (Cracknell, 1994) and learned helplessness develops (Seligman, 1975), the individual feeling that they have no control over events or their future (Rotter, 1975).

Particular goal orientations have been explored: performance and learning (Diener and Dweck, 1978, 1980; Dweck and Elliott, 1983; Elliott and Dweck, 1988). Performance goals are concerned with gaining positive judgements of competence in comparison with others: for instance being the best, outperforming others. They also include avoiding negative comparisons: for instance appearing inferior or looking stupid. In contrast, learning goals are concerned with increasing mastery, reflecting the desire to learn new skills, master new tasks or understand new things. There is a relationship between students' theories of intelligence and their goal choices. Where students hold an entity theory of intelligence (fixed and immutable), they are more likely to adopt performance goals, while those holding an incremental view of intelligence are more likely to choose a learning goal (Dweck and Leggett, 1988). Exploring the relationships between entity and incremental theories of intelligence, confidence, reactions to failure and school grades, Henderson and Dweck (1990) and Sorich and Dweck (2000) found that students who had a fixed view of intelligence performed less well than those with an incremental view, even when the latter had low confidence in their ability. Those with entity theories also tended to minimise the amount of time they put into their school work (Maehr and Midgely, 1996) and believed that if they did not have sufficient ability, hard work would not compensate (Stipek and Gralinski, 1996). Being good at something was taken as an indication that they did not need to work at it (Mueller and Dweck, 1998). Some students have been shown to self-handicap – deliberately make no effort on difficult tasks to protect their beliefs about their ability (Berglas and Jones, 1978).

The perceived value of any particular learning task depends on its relationship to personal goals, self-efficacy, the costs of undertaking it in relation to the self, and time costs in relation to other goals (Eccles, 1983). Some tasks may be perceived as enjoyable for their own sake (intrinsically motivating), or motivating because of their close relationship to developing identity and personal goals. Other tasks may be valued only because they are a means to achieve a particular end, perhaps a requirement for further study. In themselves they are not motivating. These are likely to be undertaken through adopting a surface approach to learning, with little intention to understand or engage with the material, the learner doing just enough to satisfy requirements (Entwistle, 1984). Some tasks may carry with them particular costs, in relation to self-esteem or time, which the learner may feel would be better spent engaged in other activities.

Maintaining self-esteem

Maintaining self-esteem is related to our need for competence (Koestner and McClelland, 1990) and achievement (to be more successful and better than others) (McClelland *et al.*, 1953; Atkinson, 1964). Need for achievement is based on two complementary elements: the motive to achieve success, which enhances the ego; and the motive to avoid failure, which involves the fear of losing face. The costs to self-esteem of engaging in tasks where the likelihood of failure is high may be too great for those with a high need for achievement to engage with them. Important in this respect is how the individual attributes success or failure – to stable or unstable, controllable or uncontrollable, internal or external factors. If failure is attributed to something which is unstable, e.g. bad luck, which may not occur in the future, expectations about future performance are likely to be unaffected. However, if failure is attributed to a stable factor, e.g. lack of ability, then there will be an expectation of continued failure (Weiner, 1986). Some causes are perceived to be within control, for instance the effort made; while others, for instance the difficulty of the task, are not. Some are internal, for instance prior knowledge; others are not, for example the quality of the teaching we receive. In this explanation of success and failure, these three elements interact with each other. Harter (1985) proposes that to maintain self-esteem what is important is 'beneffectance' – the individual attributing successful outcomes to internal causes and unsuccessful outcomes to external causes. Individuals with high levels of 'beneffectance' tend to perform better on academic tasks. An alternative is strategy attribution (Clifford, 1986), where failure is explained by a lack of specific strategies or skills rather than effort or general ability. This may be the most effective way of attributing success or failure to maintain motivation.

Self-efficacy

When individuals commence a task, they form expectations about how well they think they will be able to carry it out. Such expectations are based on previous performance. This is known as self-efficacy (Bandura, 1977). Efficacy beliefs have been demonstrated to be important in many aspects of human behaviour, including giving up smoking, sticking to diets and exercise routines, and academic achievement (Bandura, 1997). The self-efficacy judgements of learners are linked to their achievement (Pajares, 1994, 1997) and are important for motivation because individuals are more likely to purposefully pursue goals that seem challenging, rewarding and attainable (Bandura, 1997). Previous mastery raises efficacy beliefs contributing to the expectation that performance will be proficient in the future. Self-efficacy is distinct from our expectations for success. Many other factors that are beyond the control of the individual may impact on expectation for success. Motivation for an activity will be at its peak when strong self-efficacy beliefs are combined with some moderate uncertainty about the outcome, i.e. when a person feels competent but challenged (Bandura, 1989).

The role of emotion in learning and motivation

Learning can be a highly emotional experience. Feelings of frustration can occur and lead to anger, inappropriate behaviour or dropout (Goodwin and Hallam, in press). Learners may feel that particular tasks are too difficult and adopt coping, rather than learning, strategies (Boekarts, 1993). Fear of failure can lead to task avoidance or deliberately not making an effort (Dweck and Leggett, 1988). Anxiety tends to lead to the adoption of a surface approach to learning (Fransson, 1977) and can lead to poor performance because preoccupation with anxiety itself interferes with normal cognitive processing (Tobias, 1985). Strong emotional responses, positive or negative, facilitate memory for specific events and may have a positive or negative effect on motivation (McGaugh, 2004). Negative experiences can lead to avoidance, while a learning experience which has evoked strong positive emotions is likely to be particularly effective in engaging interest. For instance, intense, aesthetic, emotional experiences initially occurring in early childhood can engender commitment to music (Sloboda, 1990, 1991; Manturzewska, 1990).

Learning itself, when interesting and successful, is intrinsically rewarding. Being able to understand and attain competence leads to personal satisfaction. In some circumstances, individuals can experience 'flow' in learning – an exhilarating feeling when engagement in an activity leads to loss of awareness of time and space (Csikszentmihalyi, 1988). For this to occur, participants must have clear goals, receive immediate feedback as the task proceeds, feel in control and not be anxious about the outcome (Csikszentmihalyi, 1996).

Lack of motivation

Across domains there is considerable agreement about what leads to persistence in learning or lack of motivation and dropout. In optional instrumental tuition, dropouts perceive themselves as less musically able, receive less family encouragement, tend to feel musically inadequate and turn to sport and other leisure activities instead of music. They also do less practice (Sloboda et al., 1996; Hallam, 1998, 2004). Positive self-perceptions of musical skills are linked to the desire to continue music education voluntarily (Frakes, 1984). Students dropping out view continuing to play as demanding too great a time cost for the relatively small rewards offered (Hurley, 1995). The evidence from a range of learning environments supports these findings. School dropouts do less homework, exert less effort in school, participate less in school activities, and have more discipline problems (Ekstrom et al., 1986). They are more likely to have poor attendance, display disruptive behaviours and exhibit early school failure (Barrington and Hendricks, 1989; Cairns et al., 1989). They frequently feel alienated and socially isolated (Finn, 1989; Newmann, 1981).

Lack of motivation is an increasing problem in formal education. In the USA there is concern about high levels of student boredom and disaffection and high dropout rates in urban areas (National Research Council and Institute of Medicine, 2004). Students report viewing school as boring or as a mere grade game where they try to get by with as little effort as possible (Burkett, 2002), with motivation declining in the higher grade levels (Eccles et al., 1984; Fredricks and Eccles, 2002). Dropout rates are particularly high amongst minority students (Rumberger, 1987). In the UK, despite a range of government initiatives in recent years, overall attendance at school has seen little improvement, with large numbers of children regularly absent (DfES, 2004a). Absenteeism increases as students progress through school and is higher in the inner cities (Grimshaw and Pratt, 1986; DfES, 2004a). Levels of exclusion, although reduced from 1997/98, continue to be high, with boys, children with Special Educational Needs and some ethnic minorities being disproportionately represented (DfES, 2004b). It continues to be difficult to recruit students from lower socio-economic groups to higher education (HESA, 2004) and those who take up opportunities to participate in formal education as mature adults tend to be those who have already been relatively successful (Fitzgerald et al., 2002). There is a substantial group of individuals whose motivation is insufficient to sustain engagement with formal learning in the short, medium and long term.

Motivation, the self and the environment

The complex interactions that occur between the environment and the individual, which influence self-development, motivation and ultimately behaviour, are set out in Figure 1. An individual's identity or self-concept represents the way he or she thinks about him/herself and his/her relationships with others (Sullivan, 1964; Rogers, 1961; Mead, 1934). Identity is developed in response to feedback received from the environment. The desire for social approval, particularly from those we admire and respect, leads us to behave in particular ways. Over time, values and beliefs leading to behaviour associated with praise are internalised. Positive feedback from others raises self-esteem, and enhances confidence. Identity develops as a result of these processes. The family has a crucial role to play in this process in the early years, but as the child's social contacts broaden, others, including teachers and peers, become important. Individuals set themselves goals, which determine their behaviour. Goals are influenced by identity, ideal and possible selves, as well as environmental factors. Behaviour is the end link in the chain but at the time of enactment it too can be influenced and changed by environmental factors. There is interaction between the environment and the individual at every level and in the long and short term. Individuals can also act upon

Interactions between individual and environmental factors in determining motivation

Individual characteristics
- Temperament
- Gender
- Age
- Socio-cultural background

Cognitive characteristics of the individual
- Metacognitive skills
- Beliefs about learning
- Prior knowledge

Malleable aspects of the self
- Identity
- Ideal self
- Possible selves
- Self-esteem
- Self-efficacy

Cognitive processes

Interpretation of input from the environment

Attributions of success and failure

The environment
- Societal demands
- Culture and subcultures
- Family
- Friends
- Educational environment

Goals and aims
- Aspirations
- Sub-goals

Motivation to learn in specific domains

Direct influences of rewards and punishments from the environment

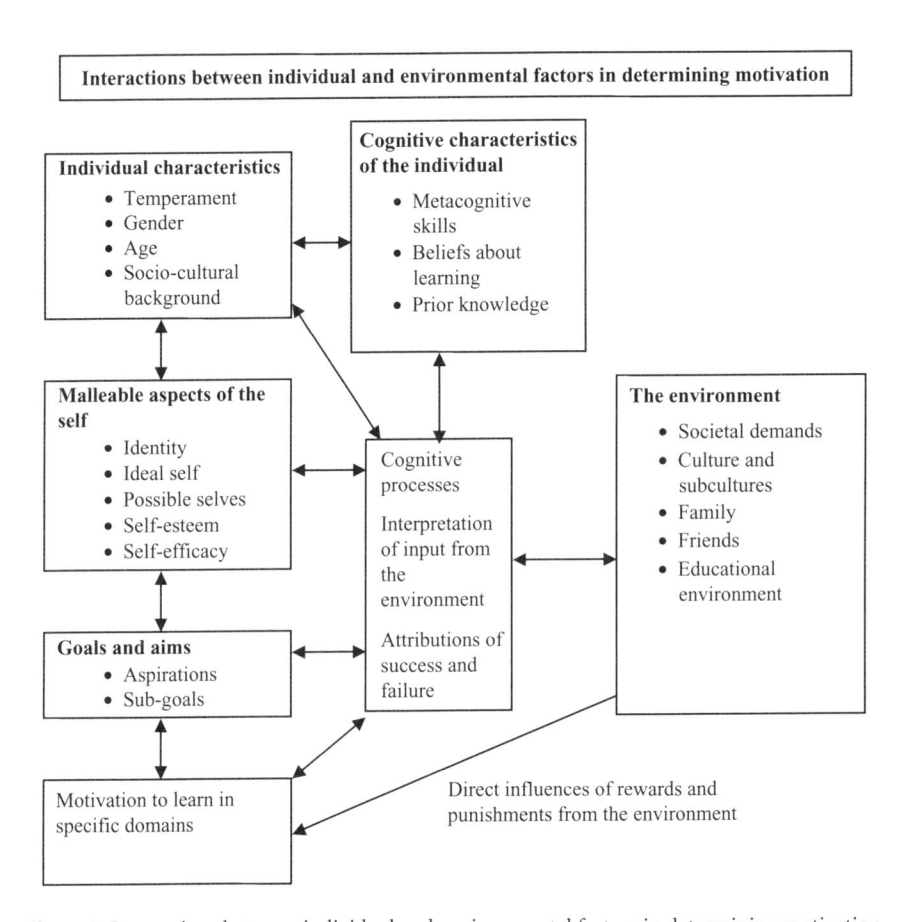

Figure 1 Interactions between individual and environmental factors in determining motivation

the environment to change it, or seek out new environments more conducive to their needs.

Behaviour is influenced by the individual's interpretation of situations and events: their expectations; and the goals that they have which mediate and regulate behaviour (Mischel, 1973). While each individual has needs and desires, these are tempered by consideration of the consequences of actions prior to attempts to satisfy them. Cognition plays a role in the ways in which we attempt to enhance our self-esteem, leading us to attribute our success or failure to causes that will allow us to maintain a consistent view of ourselves. When a learner has completed a learning task successfully, this will have an impact on self-esteem and motivation, which will be carried forward to subsequent learning tasks. Conversely, when learning outcomes are negative, motivation is usually, but not always, impaired.

Enhancing motivation to learn

There are complex interactions between learning and motivation. The more successful and enjoyable our learning in a domain, the more likely we are to be motivated to continue engaging with it. At the same time, the more interested and motivated we are in a domain, the more likely we are to persist when we fail or face difficulties, particularly if we believe that ultimately we can be successful. If early engagement with learning in a particular domain is enjoyable and positively rewarded, self-efficacy beliefs are supported; learning continues, bringing further rewards; and a 'positive possible self' develops in that domain, enhancing motivation and increasing persistence for the future. Motivation to learn is related to identity and the goals individuals set for themselves in the short, medium and long term. The value attached to learning tasks is related to the extent to which they support this developing identity and the goals derived from it. In domains where students are highly motivated, they typically adopt a deep approach to studying. Where subjects and tasks are valued only for their perceived usefulness in attaining other goals, encouraging students to learn for understanding requires the provision of interesting tasks at an appropriate level to provide challenge, but not so difficult as to be perceived as unattainable. Throughout life an individual will engage with learning across several domains and it is inevitable that they will be more successful and interested in some domains than others and that some will be more closely linked with their personal goals. From time to time personal goals may be in conflict and individuals may have to make choices based on their relative importance. The difficulty during the years of compulsory schooling, and on occasion after that when individuals may be required to undertake further training, is that in these circumstances the individual's freedom to choose what and how to learn is removed. The curriculum and often the methods of engagement with it are predetermined. If there is little relationship between personal goals and those determined by the educational system and teachers working within it, then motivation is likely to be poor. The more closely the goals of learners, teachers and educational systems are matched, the more likely that effective learning will occur.

The role of the teacher

There are a number of very practical ways in which teachers can support learning and enhance motivation. Learners, at all levels of developing expertise, need to have clear mental representations of what they are trying to achieve in relation to both processes and outcomes. It is the teacher's role to provide these in whatever form is appropriate. Learners also require feedback, either derived from self-monitoring, or from formative assessment provided by peers or teachers. The value of formative assessment for enhancing attainment and motivating learning cannot be overstated (Hallam *et al.*, 2004). Developing metacognitive skills is also crucial to facilitate independence in, and responsibility for, learning as expertise develops in the long term.

Successful completion of any task is in itself rewarding. Success can only be attained if tasks are set with regard to prior levels of attainment. During compulsory schooling there is evidence that this is often not the case (Hallam and Ireson, in press). When tasks are too difficult or the pace is too fast, the outcome is frustration because learners cannot develop deep understanding. In these circumstances, learners may adopt inefficient rote learning practices which do not provide a solid basis on which to further develop expertise, or they may abandon the task, which might have consequences for behaviour. Alternatively, work may be set at a level which is perceived as too easy or a pace which is too slow, leading to boredom, lack of challenge and reduced motivation. Grouping pupils by ability does not seem to adequately address this issue (Hallam and Ireson, in press). Allowing pupils to self-select their learning level, giving them control, in consultation with teachers where necessary, seems to successfully overcome this problem (Ireson, 1999). Enabling students to provide feedback to teachers on the depth of understanding attained in particular topics has been found to be effective in helping teachers to assess when understanding has been achieved (Hallam *et al.*, 2004), as has providing students with opportunities to engage with learning materials at different levels of complexity and opportunities to work at their own pace (Hughes, 1993).

Developing automaticity in cognitive skills takes considerable amounts of time. In those basic skills where it is desirable that everyone acquires automaticity, for instance reading and writing, learners need to be motivated to engage with relevant activities for substantial periods of time. Motivating learners to undertake such activities is best achieved by allowing them choice in selecting particular reading and writing tasks which are appropriate to meet personal goals in areas of their interest. This gives them control over the learning process and enhances motivation. For instance, it is better for children to choose to spend time reading comics than not to read at all, while adults developing basic skills will be more motivated if they can focus on attaining their own goals, whether these relate to reading a newspaper or completing job application forms, than those set by others. Being able to focus on personal goals enhances motivation and, providing that sufficient time is spent engaged with relevant activities, unless the individual has specific learning difficulties, automaticity will develop.

Much learning occurs without our conscious awareness. This implicit learning contributes to our developing knowledge base, which in turn facilitates deep understanding and further learning. For instance, our use of language can be increased as much through listening and engagement in discussion as through reading or writing. Listening to music enables us to learn the musical syntax of our culture, providing mental representations against which compositions or performances can be assessed. Engaging in a wide variety of learning experiences which may not at first sight appear to be of specific value can, through learning without conscious awareness, contribute to developing expertise. Such activities may be formal or informal and undertaken individually or as part of a group. To enhance the development of expertise, those involved in teaching should encourage all types of engagement with learning, not only those related to assessment.

Teachers should not underestimate the role that the emotions play in learning. Fear and anxiety are poor motivators and generally discourage deep learning, the development of understanding, and long-term retention. Where learning activities are interesting, enjoyable and challenging, they are more likely to lead to long-term retention, particularly where they lead to a successful outcome. Teachers also have a crucial role in offering praise for success and appropriate support (moral and practical) when a learner is faced with failure, to improve performance for the future.

To summarise, the role of the teacher in the learning process, at any educational level, is to ensure that students understand what is required, to provide appropriate opportunities for feedback, to support the development of metacognition and to motivate their students so that they want to learn. Those engaged in teaching will enhance motivation and improve learning if they:

- explain the relevance of the curriculum and specific tasks within it to students;
- avoid overloading the curriculum;
- where possible, allow students choice in what and how they learn;
- recognise that understanding is essential for learning and that understanding and learning take time;
- provide clear explanations or models of what is to be learned and how it is to be learned;
- set tasks which are challenging but not too difficult;
- provide materials and opportunities for learning which allow for different levels of prior knowledge;
- engage in formative assessment procedures with learners utilising self-, peer and teacher assessment;
- avoid making attributions related to ability;
- praise successful attainment of goals;
- encourage learners to take responsibility for their own learning.

Perhaps most important is that teachers are enthusiastic about what they are teaching: acting as role models and providing inspiration for their pupils. Where teachers operate within educational systems which place heavy constraints on what they teach and the way that they teach it, they may lose their enthusiasm or have their freedom to enhance the motivation and learning of their students curtailed. The problem for educational systems is how to reconcile the needs of society with those of the individual to the benefit of both.

The role of educational systems in enhancing motivation and learning

The development of personal identity and future 'possible selves' is highly influenced by the family. Interests which influence future career or leisure activities, and constraints placed on aspirations, tend to develop initially within the family environment. While some families are aware of the extent and power of their influence in relation to their child's future and provide opportunities for exploration of a wide range of different activities, others are not. Where this is the case, other opportunities need to be provided for children to explore where their interests might lie. Although the interests of some children may not be academic, success and satisfaction in learning in a non-academic domain can enhance self-esteem and develop a 'possible self' which provides the basis for positive personal development in general. If we wish our children to become active and successful learners, they have to believe that they are able to learn. We need to ensure that every child, at an early age, develops a positive self-concept in relation to learning in at least one subject domain. They must be able to pursue this throughout their compulsory education and beyond, and be valued for doing so. The five-year plan for education acknowledges this and proposes more choice within the curriculum, and more school clubs, outside visitors and trips. These are important. The evidence from instrumental music, where participation is voluntary, suggests that high levels of commitment, sufficient to sustain participation into secondary school and beyond, either to professional level or amateur participation in adult or senior years, is best sustained when interest is developed early on.

An individual's identity encompasses a perception of him/herself as an academic learner. Those perceiving themselves as successful in academic work have high levels of academic self-esteem and positive attitudes towards school (Ireson *et al.*, 2001). For students whose self-efficacy and expectations for academic success are low, identity and motivation will have a different focus. Unless education systems recognise and value the individual for what they can do, identity within the school environment may develop negatively and lead to alienation from school and, ultimately, from society. These feelings can be exacerbated by formal education systems which are selective in nature (see Hallam, 2002; Ireson and Hallam, 2001). The impact of this for learning is demonstrated clearly by research exploring pupils' self-perceptions prior to and after one year of being ability-grouped. There were marked differences in reported self-efficacy between pupils allocated to top and middle bands after one year, despite the fact that many had received the same test marks when allocation to groups was made. There were also changes in all pupils from incremental to entity theories of intelligence (McManus, 2002), with consequences for aspirations and motivation.

There is considerable evidence that those who are not successful academically value education but feel let down by a system which denies them opportunities to succeed (Hallam *et al.*, 2003). While opportunities for greater diversity in the range of subjects studied are being implemented, an even more fully modular system for education post-14 and beyond is necessary, to enable learners to progress to higher levels of expertise in their chosen specialisms without disruption to their learning. Our current education system does not provide a seamless progression for individuals either in relation to opportunity to learn or assessment. Each educational phase operates idiosyncratically, taking little, if any, account of the learners' previous experiences or knowledge. More flexible systems, based on prior attainment, are needed, which enable individuals of any age to move in and out of education when they are motivated to do so, either through personal interest or the needs of their employers.

A first step towards developing an education system for learning throughout life which reconciles the needs of the individual and society is to re-conceptualise learning as an ongoing process of the development of expertise, so moving away from the notion of education as an ongoing process of selection by ability to one which encourages and rewards individual effort. Adopting mastery approaches to learning, where learners aim to improve on their previous performance and continue to develop their knowledge and skills without reference to the progress of other learners, enhances motivation. Performance at any one time is merely a reflection of what has been learned to date, rather than indicating any permanent limitation on what might be achieved. This enables learners to view success in their own terms. In contrast, conceptions of learning based on ability encourage comparisons and inevitably lead some pupils to be labelled as failures, with a consequent impact on their motivation. The emphasis on age-related assessment in compulsory education exacerbates this situation. Children enter compulsory schooling with vastly different prior learning experiences. When these are conceptualised in relation to ability, children, parents and teachers develop expectations regarding future prospects that frequently become self-fulfilling. The overwhelming evidence that summer-born children tend to perform less well throughout the educational system, often being placed in low-ability groups, suggests that relatively small differences in the amount of time spent in learning prior to attending school can have a major impact on subsequent attainment in a comparative age-related system (see Hallam 2002 for a review). Outside formal education, individuals of very different ages learn and work successfully together, benefiting from their different perspectives and experiences. More age flexibility in formal education systems might also be a useful way of facilitating greater curriculum choice.

One of the most effective ways to enhance motivation is to harness the power of assessment procedures. The effects of assessment are such that Elton and Laurillard (1979) have suggested that changing assessment systems is the most effective way to change student learning. Many learning activities which take place outside compulsory education are linked to assessment systems that are designed to enable individuals to progress seamlessly to higher levels of expertise, demonstrating their level of achievement as they do so. Graded examinations in instrumental music and ballet enable students of any age to enter for a practical examination, providing motivation and a public demonstration of attainment. Similar systems are found in a range of domains, including sport, languages and computer games. What these systems have in common is that they provide individuals with challenge and opportunities to demonstrate achievement when they have reached the appropriate level of expertise to attain them. There are no age constraints. In addition, these assessment systems are generally 'authentic', in that they focus on assessing the particular expertise being acquired. An all-encompassing assessment system setting levels from beginner to the highest levels of expertise across a range of domains (vocational and academic) would enable all students to demonstrate what they had achieved. To promote motivation in the early stages, the levels would need to be attained within relatively short time spaces, but as expertise and commitment developed, the time needed to attain higher levels could be increased. At a practical level, cost-effectiveness could be maintained through a combination of computer and teacher assessments. External bodies could provide rigorous quality assurance at particular levels equivalent to current existing examinations. The qualifications would be transparent and portable. Each phase of education and the institutions within it would be able to set the levels required for particular courses of study. Existing recognised qualifications would be designated as being at particular levels, so there would be no threat to their integrity or standards. The advantages of such a system would be to provide greater motivation and an ongoing record of progress for every area of learning with which the individual wished to engage. Learners of any age would be able to demonstrate attainment at any level in any domain, enabling those with higher levels of prior knowledge to be assessed at earlier ages and adult returners to education to slot in at the level they had achieved before completing compulsory education. The 'backwash' from such an assessment system would transform our educational system, enhancing student motivation and promoting learning.

If we truly wish individuals to engage with formal learning throughout the lifespan, we have to find ways of motivating them to engage with learning from an early age and maintain that engagement. This requires that our educational system provides more rewarding learning experiences for all learners. This can be achieved through:

- offering interesting, challenging work, set at an appropriate level which is perceived to be relevant to personal learning goals;
- providing clear models of processes and learning outcomes;
- providing opportunities for feedback on progress and outcomes;
- rewarding success through praise and an appropriate assessment system.

To attain these aims, our educational system needs to be more flexible, responsive to individual needs and able to offer continuity and seamless progression.

References

Akin, O. (1980) *Models of Architectural Knowledge*. London: Pion.
Alexander, P.A. (2003) 'The development of expertise: the journey from acclimation to proficiency'. *Educational Researcher*, 32(8), 10–14.
Alexander, P.A., Sperl, C.T., Buehl, M.M., Fives, H. and Chiu, S. (in press) *Modeling domain learning: Profiles from the field of special education*.
Altenmuller, E.O. (2003) 'How many music centres are in the brain?' In I. Peretz and R. Zatorre (eds), *The Cognitive Neuroscience of Music*. Oxford: Oxford University Press, 346–56.
Altenmuller, E.O., Gruhn, W., Parlitz, D. *et al.* (1997) 'Music learning produces changes in brain activation patterns: a longitudinal DC-EEG-study unit'. *International Journal of Arts Medicine*, 5, 28–34.
Atkinson, J. (1964) *An Introduction to Motivation*. New York: D. Van Nostrand.
Bandura, A. (1977) 'Self-efficacy: Toward a unifying theory of behavioural change'. *Psychological Review*, 84, 191–215.
Bandura, A. (1989) 'Self-regulation of motivation and action through internal standards and goal systems'. In L.A. Pervin (ed.), *Goal Concepts in Personality and Social Psychology*. Hillsdale, NJ: Erlbaum.
Bandura, A. (1997) *Self-Efficacy: The exercise of control*. New York: Free Press.
Barnes, D. (1976) *From Communication to Curriculum*. Harmondsworth: Penguin Educational.
Barrington, B.L. and Hendricks, B. (1989) 'Differentiating characteristics of high school graduates, dropouts and nongraduates'. *Journal of Educational Research*, 82, 309–19.
Bastian, H.G. (1989) *Leben für Musik. Eine Biographie-Studie über musikalische (Hoch)-Begabungen*. Mainz, Germany: Schott.
Belz, M.J.D. (1995) 'The German *Gesangverein* as a model of life long participation in music'. Doctoral dissertation, University of Minnesota, 1994. *Dissertation Abstracts International*, 56, 485A.
Berglas, S. and Jones, E.E. (1978) 'Drug choice as a self-handicapping strategy in response to non-contingent success'. *Journal of Personality and Social Psychology*, 36, 405–17.
Biggs, J.B. and Telfer, R. (1987) *The Process of Learning* (2nd edition). Sydney: Prentice Hall of Australia.
Blakemore, S.J. and Frith, U. (2000) *The Implications of Recent Developments in Neuroscience for Research on Teaching and Learning*. London: Institute of Cognitive Neuroscience.
Boekarts, M. (1993) 'Being concerned with well-being and with learning'. *Educational Psychologist*, 28(2), 149–67.

Borthwick, S.J. and Davidson, J.W. (2002) 'Developing a child's identity as a musician: a family "script" perspective'. In R.A.R. MacDonald, D.J. Hargreaves and D. Miell (eds), *Musical Identities*. Oxford: Oxford University Press, 60–78.

Burkett, E. (2002) *Another Planet: A year in the life of a suburban high school*. New York: Harper Collins.

Cairns, R.B., Cairns, B.D. and Neckerman, H.J. (1989) 'Early school dropout: Configurations and determinants'. *Child Development*, 60, 1437–52.

Chase, W.G. and Simon, H.A. (1973) 'Perception in chess'. *Cognitive Psychology*, 4, 55–81.

Chi, M.T.H., Feltovitch, P.J. and Glaser, R. (1981) 'Categorisation and representation of physics problems by experts and novices'. *Cognitive Science*, 5, 121–5.

Chi, M.T.H., Glaser, R. and Rees, E. (1982) 'Expertise in problem solving'. In R. Sternberg (ed.), *Advances in the Psychology of Human Intelligence*. Vol. 1. Hillsdale, NJ: Lawrence Erlbaum Associates, 117–76.

Chiodo, P.A. (1998) 'The development of lifelong commitment: a qualitative study of adult instrumental music participation'. Doctoral dissertation, State University of New York at Buffalo, 1997. *Dissertation Abstracts International*, 58(7), 2578A.

Clifford, M.M. (1986) 'The comparative effects of strategy and effort attributions'. *British Journal of Educational Psychology*, 56, 75–83.

Collins, D. (2005) 'A synthesis process model of creative thinking in composition'. *Psychology of Music*, 33(2), 193–216.

Conda, J.M. (1997) 'The late bloomers piano club: A case study of a group in progress'. Unpublished doctoral dissertation, University of Oklahoma. *Dissertation Abstracts International*, 58, 409A.

Cracknell, D.J. (1994) 'Possible selves and adolescents: reality or fantasy?' Unpublished master's dissertation, Institute of Education, University of London.

Csikszentmihalyi, M. (1988) 'Society, culture and person: a systems view of creativity'. In R.J. Sternberg (ed.), *The Nature of Creativity*. New York: Cambridge University Press, 325–39.

Csikszentmihalyi, M. (1996) *Creativity*. New York: Harper Collins.

Davidson, J., Howe, M. and Sloboda, J. (1995) 'What motivates instrumental learning'. Paper presented at the VIIth European Conference on Developmental Psychology, Krakow, 23–27 August.

DeGroot, A. (1966) 'Perception and memory versus thought: some old ideas and recent findings'. In B. Kleinmuntz (ed.), *Problem Solving*. New York: Wiley, 19–50.

DfES (Department for Education and Skills) (2004a) *Pupil Absence in Schools in England 2003/04*. London: DfES.

DfES (Department for Education and Skills) (2004b) *Permanent Exclusions from Maintained Schools in England 2002/03*. London: DfES.

Diener, C.I. and Dweck, C.S. (1978) 'An analysis of learned helplessness: continuous changes in performance, strategy and achievement cognitions following failure'. *Journal of Personality and Social Psychology*, 36, 451–62.

Diener, C.I. and Dweck, C.S. (1980) 'An analysis of learned helplessness: (II) The processing of success'. *Journal of Personality and Social Psychology*, 39, 940–52.

Dowling, W.J. (1992) 'Perceptual grouping, attention and expectancy in listening to music'. In J. Sundberg (ed.), *Gluing Tones: grouping in music composition, performance and listening*. Stockholm: Publications of the Royal Swedish Academy, 77–98.

Dowling, W.J. (1993) 'Procedural and declarative knowledge in music cognition and education'. In T.J. Tighe and W.J. Wilding (eds), *Psychology and Music: The understanding of melody and rhythm*. Hillsdale, N.J.: Erlbaum, 5–18.

Dweck, C.S. and Elliott, E.S. (1983) 'Achievement motivation'. In P. Mussen and E.M. Hetherington (eds), *Handbook of Child Psychology*. New York: Wiley.

Dweck, C.S. and Leggett, E.L. (1988) 'A social cognitive approach to motivation and personality'. *Psychological Review*, 95(2), 256–373.

Eccles, J. (1983) 'Expectancies, values and academic behaviours'. In J.T. Spence (ed.), *Achievement and Achievement Motives*. San Francisco: Freeman.

Eccles, J.S., Midgley, C. and Adler, T.F. (1984) 'Grade-related changes in school environment: effects on achievement motivation'. In J.G. Nicholls (ed.), *Advances in Motivation and Achievement*. Greenwich CT: JAI Press, 283–331.

Egan, D.E. and Schwartz, B.J. (1979) 'Chunking in recall of symbolic drawings'. *Memory and Cognition*, 7, 149–58.

Ekstrom, R.B., Goertz, M.E., Pollack, J.M. and Rock, D.A. (1986) 'Who drops out of high school and why? Findings from a national study'. *Teachers College Record*, 87, 356–73.

Elbert, T., Pantev, C., Wienbruch, C., Rockstroh, B. and Taub, E. (1995) 'Increased cortical representation of the fingers of the left hand in string players'. *Science*, 270, 305–6.

Elliott, E.S. and Dweck, C.S. (1988) 'Goals: an approach to motivation and achievement'. *Journal of Personality and Social Psychology*, 54, 5–12.

Elton, L.B.R. and Laurillard, D. (1979) 'Trends in student learning'. *Studies in Higher Education*, 4, 87–102.

Entwistle, N. (1984) 'Contrasting perspectives on learning'. In F. Marton, D. Hounsell and N. Entwistle (eds), *The Experience of Learning*. Edinburgh: Scottish Academic Press, 1–18.

Ericsson, K.A. and Chase, W.G. (1982) 'Exceptional memory'. *American Scientist*, 6, 607–12.

Fields, R.D. (2005) 'Making memories stick'. *Scientific American*, February, 75–81.
Finn, J.D. (1989) 'Withdrawing from school'. *Review of Educational Research*, 59, 117–42.
Finnas, L. (1987) 'Do young people misjudge each other's musical taste?' *Psychology of Music*, 15, 152–66.
Finnas, L. (1989) 'A comparison between young people's privately and publicly expressed musical preferences'. *Psychology of Music*, 17, 132–45.
Fitts, P.M. and Posner, M.I. (1967) *Human Performance*. Belmont, CA: Brooks Cole.
Fitzgerald, R., Taylor, R. and La Valle, I. (2002) *National Adult Learning Survey*. London: DfES.
Frakes, L. (1984) 'Differences in music achievement, academic achievement and attitude among participants, dropouts and non-participants in secondary school music'. Unpublished PhD thesis, University of Iowa.
Fransson, A. (1977) 'On qualitative differences in learning IV: effects of motivation and test anxiety on process and outcome'. *British Journal of Educational Psychology*, 47, 244–57.
Fredricks, J.A. and Eccles, J.S. (2002) 'Children's competence and value beliefs from childhood to adolescence: growth trajectories in two "male-typed" domains'. *Journal of Developmental Psychology*, 38, 519–33.
Glaser, R. and Chi, M.T.H. (1988) 'Overview'. In M.T.H. Chi, R. Glaser and M.J. Farr (eds), *The Nature of Expertise*. Hillsdale, NJ: Lawrence Erlbaum Associates, xv–xxviii.
Goodwin, T. and Hallam, S. (in press) 'Adult Learning: the role of emotional intelligence'. In P. Sutherland and J. Crowther (eds), *Lifelong Learning: Concepts and contexts*. London: RoutledgeFalmer.
Goolsby, T.W. (1994) 'Profiles of processing: eye movements during sightreading'. *Music Perception*, 12, 97–123.
Grimshaw, R.H. and Pratt, J.D. (1986) 'Counting the absent scholars: some implications for managerial practice arising from a survey of absenteeism in a city's secondary schools'. *School Organisation*, 6(1), 155–73.
Hallam, S. (1995) 'Professional musicians' orientations to practice: implications for teaching'. *British Journal of Music Education*, 12(1), 3–19.
Hallam, S. (1998) 'Predictors of achievement and drop out in instrumental tuition'. *Psychology of Music*, 26(2), 116–32.
Hallam, S. (2001) 'The development of metacognition in musicians: implications for education'. *The British Journal of Music Education*, 18(1), 27–39.
Hallam, S. (2001b) 'The development of expertise in young musicians: strategy use, knowledge acquisition and individual diversity'. *Music Education Research*, 3(1), 7–23.

Hallam, S. (2002) *Ability Grouping in Schools: A Literature Review*. London: Institute of Education, University of London.

Hallam, S. (2004) 'How important is practicing as a predictor of learning outcomes in instrumental music?' In S.D. Lipscomb, R. Ashley, R.O. Gjerdingen and P. Webster (eds), *Proceedings of the 8th International Conference on Music Perception and Cognition, August 3–7 2004*. Northwestern University, Evanston, 165–68.

Hallam, S. and Ireson, J. (in press) 'Secondary school pupils' satisfaction with their ability group placements'. *British Educational Research Journal*.

Hallam, S. and Prince, V. (2000) *Research into Instrumental Music Services*. London: Department for Education and Employment.

Hallam, S. and Rogers, L. with Rhamie, J., Shaw, J., Rees, E., Haskins, H., Blackmore, J. and Hallam, J. (2003) *Evaluation of Skill Force*. London: Institute of Education, University of London.

Hallam, S., Kirton. A., Peffers, J., Robertson, P. and Stobart, G. (2004) *Final Report of the Evaluation of Project 1 of the Assessment is for Learning Development Programme: Support for professional practice in formative assessment. Final Report*. Edinburgh: Scottish Executive.

Harnischmacher, C. (1995). 'Spiel oder Arbeit? Eine Pilotstudie zu, instrumentalen Uberverhalten von Kindern und Jugendlichen'. In H. Gembris, R.D. Kraemer and G. Maas (eds), *Musikpadagogische Forschungsberichte 1994*. Augsburg: Wisner, 41–56.

Harter, S. (1985) 'Competence as a dimension of self-evaluation: toward a comprehension model of self-worth'. In R. Leahy (ed.), *The Development of the Self*. New York: Academic.

Henderson, V. and Dweck, C.S. (1990) 'Achievement and motivation in adolescence: a new model and data'. In S. Feldman and G. Elliott (eds), *At the Threshold: The developing adolescent*. Cambridge, MA: Harvard University Press.

HESA (Higher Education Statistics Agency) (2004) *Performance Indicators in Higher Education in the UK 2002/03*. Online. Available http://www.hesa.ac.uk.

Hinds, S. (2005) 'Perceived causes of male African-Caribbean underachievement in the United Kingdom'. Unpublished master's dissertation, Institute of Education, University of London.

Holmquist, S.P. (1995) 'A study of community choir members' school experiences'. Unpublished doctoral dissertation, University of Oregon. *Dissertation Abstracts International*, 56, 1699A.

Howe, M. and Sloboda, J. (1991) 'Young musicians' accounts of significant influences in their early lives. 2. Teachers, practising and performing'. *British Journal of Music Education*, 8(1), 53–63.

Howe, M.J.A., Davidson, J.W., Moore, D.M. and Sloboda, J.A. (1995) 'Are there early childhood signs of musical ability?' *Psychology of Music*, 23, 162–76.

Hughes, D. (1993) *Flexible Learning: Evidence examined*. Stafford: Network Educational Press Ltd.

Hurley, C.G. (1995) 'Student motivations for beginning and continuing/discontinuing string music tuition'. *The Quarterly Journal of Music Teaching and Learning*, 6(1), 44–55.

Ireson, J. (1999) *Innovative Grouping Practices in Secondary Schools*. London: Department for Education and Employment.

Ireson, J. and Hallam, S. (2001) *Ability Grouping in Education*. London: Sage Publications.

Ireson, J., Hallam, S. and Plewis, I. (2001) 'Ability grouping in secondary schools: effects on pupils' self-concepts'. *British Journal of Educational Psychology*, 71, 315–26.

Jetton, T.L. and Alexander, P.A. (1997) 'Instructional importance: what teachers value and what students learn'. *Reading Research Quarterly*, 32, 290–308.

Kagan, D. (1988) 'Teaching as clinical problem solving: a critical examination of the analogy and its implications'. *Review of Educational Research*, 58, 482–505.

Karni, A., Meyer, G., Jezzard, P., Adams, M.M., Turner, R. and Ungerleider, L.G. (1995) 'FMRI evidence for adult motor cortex plasticity during motor skill learning'. *Nature*, 377, 155–8.

Kember, D. (1997) 'A reconceptualisation of research into university academics' conceptions of teaching'. *Learning and Instruction*, 7(3), 255–75.

Kemp, A.E. (1996) *The Musical Temperament: Psychology and personality of musicians*. Oxford: Oxford University Press.

Koestner, R. and McClelland, D.C. (1990) 'Perspectives on competence motivation'. In L. Pervin (ed.), *Handbook of Personality: Theory and research*. New York: Guilford Press.

Koupadi, S. (1995) 'Possible selves: relationships with motivation, study skills and the self-concept in Greek students'. Unpublished master's dissertation, Institute of Education, University of London.

Lamont, A. (2002) 'Musical identities and the school environment'. In R.A.R. MacDonald, D.J. Hargreaves and D. Miell (eds), *Musical Identities*. Oxford: Oxford University Press, 41–59.

Larkin, J.H. (1983) 'The role of problem representation in physics'. In D. Gentner and A.L. Stevens (eds), *Mental Models*. Hillsdale, NJ: Lawrence Erlbaum Associates, 75–100.

Larson, P. (1983) 'An exploratory study of lifelong musical interest and activity: case studies of twelve retired adults'. Unpublished doctoral dissertation, Temple University, 1982. *Dissertation Abstracts International*, 44, 100A.

Lassiter, D.G. (1981) 'A survey of parental involvement in the development of professional musicians'. Unpublished master's thesis, Florida State University, Tallahassee.

Leinhardt, G. (1990) 'Capturing craft knowledge in teaching'. *Educational Researcher*, 19(2), 18–25.

Leinhardt, G. and Greeno, J.G. (1986) 'The cognitive skill of teaching'. *Journal of Educational Psychology*, 78, 75–95.

Maehr, M.L. and Midgely, C. (1996) *Transforming School Cultures.* Boulder, CO: Westview Press.

Maguire, E.A., Gadian, D.G., Johnsrude, I.S., Good, C.D., Ashburner, J., Frackowiak, R. and Frith, C.D. (2000) 'Navigation-related structural change in the hippocampi of taxi drivers'. *Proceedings of the National Academy of Sciences of the United States of America*, 97(8), 4398–4403.

Manturzewska, M. (1990) 'A biographical study of the life-span development of professional musicians'. *Psychology of Music*, 18(2), 112–39.

Markus, H. and Ruvolo, A. (1989) 'Possible selves: Personalized representations of goals'. In L.A. Pervin (ed.), *Goal Concepts in Personality and Social Psychology*. Hillsdale, NJ: Lawrence Erlbaum Associates.

McClelland, D.C., Atkinson, J.W., Clark, R.W. and Lowell, E.L. (1953) *The Achievement Motive.* New York: Appleton-Century-Crofts.

McGaugh, J.L. (2004) 'The amygdale modulates the consolidation of memories of emotionally arousing experiences'. *Annual Review of Neuroscience*, 27, 1–28.

McManus, J. (2002) 'The impact of a banding system on pupils' learning'. Unpublished report, St Joseph's School, South Tyneside.

Mead, G.H. (1934) *Mind, Self and Society.* Chicago: University of Chicago Press.

Mischel, W. (1973) 'Toward a cognitive social learning reconceptualisation of personality'. *Psychological Review*, 80, 252–83.

Mueller, C.M. and Dweck, C.S. (1998) 'Intelligence praise can undermine motivation and performance'. *Journal of Personality and Social Psychology*, 75, 33–52.

Munte, T.F., Nager, W., Beiss, T., Schroeder, C. and Erne, S.N. (2003) 'Specialization of the specialised electrophysiological investigations in professional musicians'. In G. Avanzini, C. Faienza, D. Minciacchi, L. Lopez, and M. Majno (eds), *The Neurosciences and Music*. New York: New York Academy of Sciences, 112–17.

National Research Council and Institute of Medicine (2004) *Engaging Schools: Fostering high school students' motivation to learn.* Washington DC: National Academy Press.

Newell, A. (1990) *Unified Theories of Cognition.* Cambridge: Cambridge University Press.

Newmann, F. (1981) 'Student engagement in academic work: expanding the perspective on secondary schooling effectiveness'. In J.R. Bliss and W.A. Firestone (eds), *Rethinking Effective Schools: Research and practice*. Englewood Cliffs, NJ: Prentice-Hall, 58–76.

Pajares, F. (1994) 'Role of self-efficacy and self-concept beliefs in mathematical problem solving: a path analysis'. *Journal of Educational Psychology*, 86, 193–203.

Pajares, F. (1997) 'Current directions in self-efficacy research'. In M.L. Maehr and P.R. Pintrich (eds), *Advances in Motivation and Achievement*. Greenwich, CT: JAI Press, 1–49.

Pantev, C., Engelien, A., Candia, V. and Elbert, T. (2003) 'Representational cortex in musicians'. In I. Peretz and R. Zatorre (eds), *The Cognitive Neuroscience of Music*. Oxford: Oxford University Press, 382–95.

Pascual-Leone, A. (2003) 'The brain that makes music and is changed by it'. In I. Peretz and R. Zatorre (eds), *The Cognitive Neuroscience of Music*. Oxford: Oxford University Press, 396–412.

Pascual-Leone, A., Grafman, J. and Hallett, M. (1994) 'Modulation of cortical motor ouput maps during development of implicit and explicit knowledge'. *Science*, 263, 1287–9.

Pratt, D. (1992) 'Conceptions of teaching'. *Adult Education Quarterly*, 42, 203–20.

Rexroad, E.F. (1985) 'Influential factors on the musical development of outstanding professional singers'. EdD thesis, University of Illinois at Urbana-Champaign.

Rogers, C.R. (1961) *On Becoming a Person*. Boston: Houghton Mifflin.

Rogoff, B. (1990) *Apprenticeship in Thinking: Cognitive development in social context*. New York: Oxford University Press.

Rotter, J. (1975) 'Some problems and misconceptions related to the construct of internal versus external control of reinforcement'. *Journal of Consulting and Clinical Psychology*, 43, 56–67.

Rumberger, R.W. (1987) 'High school dropouts: a review of issues and evidence'. *Review of Educational Research*, 57, 101–21.

Seligman, M.E.P. (1975) *Helplessness: On depression, development and death*. San Francisco: Freeman.

Sloboda, J.A. (1984) 'Experimental studies of music reading: a review'. *Music Perception*, 2, 222–36.

Sloboda, J.A. (1990) 'Music as a language'. In F. Wilson and F. Roehmann (eds), *Music and child development*. St Louis, Missouri: MMB Inc.

Sloboda, J. (1991) 'Music structure and emotional response: Some empirical findings'. *Psychology of Music*, 19(2), 110–120.

Sloboda, J.A. and Davidson, J. (1996) 'The young performing musician'. In I. Deliege and J.A. Sloboda (eds), *Musical Beginnings: Origins and development of musical competence.* Oxford: Oxford University Press.

Sloboda, J.A. and Howe, M.J.A. (1991) 'Biographical precursors of musical excellence: an interview study'. *Psychology of Music,* 19, 3–21.

Sloboda, J.A., Davidson, J.W., Howe, M.J.A. and Moore, D.G. (1996) 'The role of practice in the development of performing musicians'. *British Journal of Psychology,* 87, 287–309.

Sorich, L. and Dweck, C.S. (2000) 'Mastery oriented thinking'. In C.R. Snyder (ed.), *Coping.* New York: Oxford University Press.

Sosniak, L. A. (1985) 'Learning to be a concert pianist: developing talent in young people'. In B.S. Bloom (ed.), *Developing Talent in Young People.* New York: Ballantine, 19–67.

Sosniak, L.A (1990) 'The tortoise and the hare and the development of talent'. In M.J.A. Howe (ed.), *Encouraging the Development of Exceptional Skills and Talents.* Leicester: The British Psychological Society.

Stipek, D.J. and Gralinski, H. (1996) 'Children's beliefs about intelligence and school performance'. *Journal of Educational Psychology,* 88, 397–407.

Sudnow, D. (1978) *Ways of the Hand: The organisation of improvised conduct.* London: Routledge and Kegan Paul.

Sullivan, H.S. (1964) *The Fusion of Psychiatry and Social Science.* New York: Norton.

Szubertowska, E. (in press) 'Education and the music culture of Polish adolescence'. *Psychology of Music.*

Tobias, S. (1985) 'Test anxiety: interference, defective skills, and cognitive capacity. *Educational Psychologist,* 20(3), 135–42.

Waters, A.J., Underwood, G. and Findlay, J.M. (1997) 'Studying expertise in music reading: use of a pattern-matching paradigm'. *Perception and Psychophysics,* 59, 477–88.

Weiner, B. (1986) *An Attributional Theory of Motivation and Emotion.* New York: Springer-Verlag.

Weiser, M. and Shertz, J. (1983) 'Programming problem representation in novice and expert programmers'. *Instructional Journal of Man–Machine Studies,* 14, 391–96.

Younker, B.A. and Smith, W.H. (1996) 'Comparing and modelling musical thought processes of expert and novice composers'. *Bulletin of the Council for Research in Music Education,* 128, 25–35.